Juliette Clarke
1990

OTHER HELEN EXLEY GIFTBOOKS:

Thank Heavens for Friends
To a very special Friend
A Little Book for a Friend
The Best of Women's Quotations
A special gift of Peace and Calm
Thank you for Every Little Thing
Thank You To a Very Special Friend
... And Wisdom Comes Quietly

Copyright © Helen Exley 2002
Selection © Helen Exley 2002
The moral right of the author has been asserted.

12 11 10 9 8 7 6 5 4 3 2 1

ISBN 1-86187-454-5

Selection and design by Helen Exley
Illustrated by Juliette Clarke
Printed in China

Exley Publications Ltd, 16 Chalk Hill, Watford, Herts, WD19 4BG, UK.
Exley Publications LLC, 232 Madison Avenue, Suite 1409, NY 10016, USA.
www.helenexleygiftbooks.com.

Acknowledgements: The publishers are grateful for permission to reproduce copyright material.
Whilst every effort has been made to trace copyright holders, the publishers would be pleased to hear from any not here acknowledged.
PAM BROWN, PAMELA DUGDALE, HELEN M. EXLEY, MARION C. GARRETTY, CHARLOTTE GRAY, STUART & LINDA MACFARLANE, CLARA ORTEGA, MAYA V. PATEL, PUSHPA PATEL, HELEN FITZWALTER-READ, HELEN THOMSON : published with permission © Helen Exley 2002.

For a real
Friend

A BOOK OF
THOUGHTFUL QUOTES

A HELEN EXLEY GIFTBOOK

EXLEY
NEW YORK • WATFORD, UK

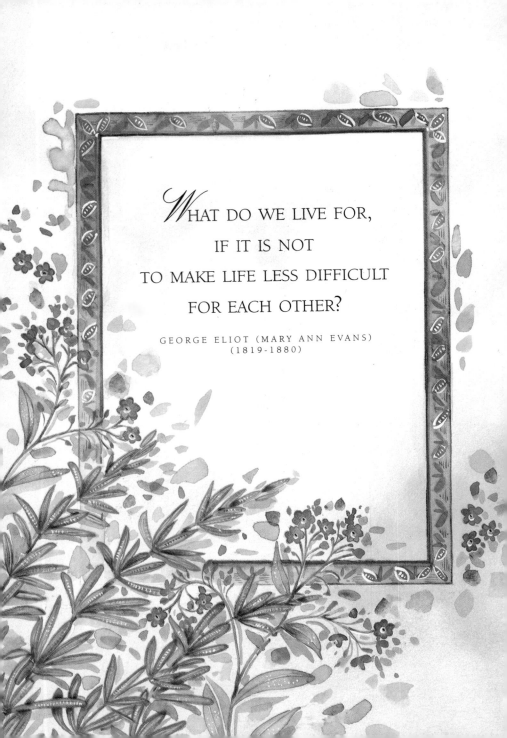

WHAT DO WE LIVE FOR,
IF IT IS NOT
TO MAKE LIFE LESS DIFFICULT
FOR EACH OTHER?

GEORGE ELIOT (MARY ANN EVANS)
(1819-1880)

There are times when I have needed
to tell someone my fear,
times when I have needed someone
to share a secret,
times when I have needed someone to rejoice
with me over an achievement.
And those are the times when only
my friend will do.

PAM BROWN, b.1928

The reward of friendship is itself.
The man who hopes for anything else does
not understand what true friendship is.

AILRED (AETHELRED) OF RIEVAULX (c.1110 -1167)

Have friends, not for the sake of receiving,
but of giving.

JOSEPH ROUX,
FROM "MEDITATIONS OF A PARISH PRIEST"

If I don't have friends, then I ain't got nothin'.

BILLIE HOLIDAY
(1915-1959)

$\mathscr{A}$s long as there is a post
and the telephone is not cut off,
so long as we have things to tell and joys
and anxieties to share –
we will be friends. Always.

MARION C. GARRETTY, b.1917

Because of a friend, life is a little stronger,
fuller, more gracious thing for the
friend's existence, whether she be near or far.
If the friend is close at hand,
that is best; but if she is far away
she still is there to think of, to wonder about,
to hear from, to write to, to share life
and experience with, to serve, to honour,
to admire, to love.

ARTHUR CHRISTOPHER BENSON (1862-1925)

A PHONE CALL IS GOOD.
BUT YOU CAN RE-READ A LETTER.

PAM BROWN, b.1928

I trust that even when I'm out of sight
I'm not out of mind.
Silences and distances are woven into
the texture of every true friendship.

ROBERTA ISRAELOFF

Yes, there is a talkability
that can express itself even without words.
There is an exchange of thought and feeling
which is happy alike in speech and in silence.
It is quietness pervaded with friendship.

HENRY VAN DYKE

That friendship only is, indeed, genuine when two friends, without speaking a word to each other, can, nevertheless, find happiness in being together.

GEORG EBERS (1837-1898)

For what do my friends stand?
Not for the clever things they say:
I do not remember them half an hour
after they are spoken.
It is always the unspoken, the unconscious,
which is their reality to me.

MARK RUTHERFORD (1831-1913)

Shout and everyone hears what you say.
Whisper and those close hear what you say.
Be silent and your best friend hears
what you say.

STUART AND LINDA MACFARLANE

Old friends disintegrate together –
which enlivens the process.

PAM BROWN, b.1928

To others, we will be seen as two
old biddies kicking off their shoes,
dumping down shopping bags,
choosing lethal pastries.
But to each other we are ourselves,
a little scarred by passing years, but still
the girls who shared a bag of toffee
on the playground wall, we at least
are not deceived by skin, spectacles
and silvery hair.

PAMELA DUGDALE

Happiness is giving a little
and taking a little,
even if it is a mere dandelion.
It is worth a bouquet of red roses
wrapped in delicate lace
if it is given with care.

HELEN CADDICK, AGE 11,
FROM "A CHILD'S VIEW OF HAPPINESS"

A JOY SHARED
IS A JOY DOUBLED.

GOETHE (1749-1832)

Grief can take care of itself,
but to get the full value out of joy
you must have someone to divide it with.

MARK TWAIN (1835-1910)

One can never speak enough of the virtues,
the dangers, the power of shared laughter.

FRANCOISE SAGAN, b.1935

EVERY GOOD THING
IS BETTER
IF YOU CAN SHARE
IT WITH A FRIEND.

PAM BROWN, b.1928

That Best Portion
Of A Good Man's Life,
His Little, Nameless,
Unremembered Acts Of Kindness
And Of Love.

WILLIAM WORDSWORTH (1770-1850)

... when people have light in themselves, it will shine out from them. Then we get to know each other as we walk together in the darkness, without needing to pass our hands over each other's faces, or to intrude into each other's hearts.

ALBERT SCHWEITZER (1875-1965)

There are red-letter days in our lives when we meet people who thrill us like a fine poem, people whose handshake is brimful of unspoken sympathy and whose sweet, rich natures impart to our eager, impatient spirits a wonderful restfulness....

HELEN KELLER (1880-1968)

FRIENDSHIP IS ALWAYS A SWEET
RESPONSIBILITY, NEVER AN OPPORTUNITY.

KAHLIL GIBRAN (1883-1931)

*The glory of friendship
is not the outstretched hand, nor
the kindly smile nor the joy of
companionship; it is the spirited inspiration
that comes to one when he discovers
that someone else believes in him
and is willing to trust him with
his friendship.*

RALPH WALDO EMERSON (1803-1882)

Friends are closest to us
who best understand what life means to us,
who feel for us as we feel for ourselves,
who are bound to us in triumph and disaster,
who break the spell of our loneliness.

HENRY ALONZO MYERS

One of the qualities I value most in a friend is discretion.
You must be able to know that you can be absolutely
frank with the person you are talking to. The privilege of
confidence binds people together, as does the mutual
vulnerability it implies.

ROBIN COOK

A friend believes in you when no one else does
— and that includes yourself,
listens when she's heard the tale before
— several times (a hundred times),
is there for you when things go wrong
— and never says I told you so,
helps to pick up the pieces
— and glue the bits together.

PAM BROWN, b.1928

$\mathcal{T}$HERE'S NOTHING WORTH
THE WEAR OF WINNING,
BUT LAUGHTER AND THE LOVE
OF FRIENDS.

HILAIRE BELLOC
(1870-1953)

Girl talk is much the same in every age,
though differing in detail. Appearance, men,
ambitions and despondencies, parents and the future.
Boasting of conquests. Dramatizing the dull.
Speculating on the half unknown. And since
the beginning, bursts of giggling – helpless laughter
at the lunacies of life. The happy silliness that keeps
the dark at bay.

PAM BROWN, b.1928

That is the best – to laugh with someone because you
both think the same things are funny.

GLORIA VANDERBILT

... A friend doesn't go on a diet because you are fat.
A friend never defends a husband who gets his wife
an electric skillet for her birthday. A friend will tell
you she saw your old boyfriend – and he's a priest.

ERMA BOMBECK, b.1927

Friends put the entire world to rights
over a cup of tea and a bun.

CHARLOTTE GRAY, b.1937

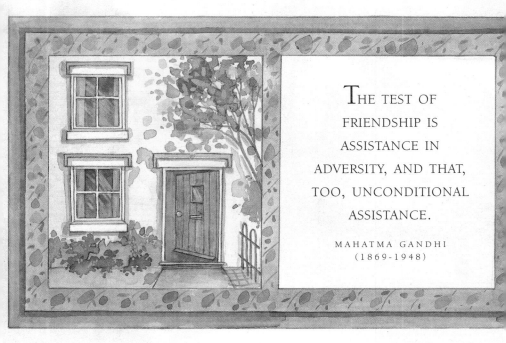

THE TEST OF
FRIENDSHIP IS
ASSISTANCE IN
ADVERSITY, AND THAT,
TOO, UNCONDITIONAL
ASSISTANCE.

MAHATMA GANDHI
(1869-1948)

IT'S NOT SO MUCH OUR FRIENDS'
HELP THAT HELPS US AS
THE CONFIDENCE AND KNOWLEDGE
THAT THEY WILL HELP US.

EPICURUS (341-270 B.C.)

Friend, whatever hardships threaten
If thou call me, I'll befriend thee. All-enduring, fearlessly,
I'll befriend thee.

OGLALA SIOUX INDIAN

A blessed thing it is for any man or woman
to have a friend; one human soul whom we can trust
utterly; who knows the best and the worst of us,
and who loves us in spite of all our faults;
who will speak the honest truth to us, while the world
flatters us to our face, and laughs behind our back;
who will give us counsel and reproof
in the day of prosperity and self-conceit;
but who, again, will comfort and encourage us
in the day of difficulty and sorrow,
when the world leaves us alone to fight our own
battle as we can.

CHARLES KINGSLEY (1819-1875)

In prosperity our friends know us;
In adversity we know our friends.

J.M. BARRIE (1860-1937)

In the darkest hours I know I can reach out
and find your hand.

PAM BROWN, b.1928

... friendship, the ease of it,
it is not something to be taken lightly —
nor for granted.
Because, after breathing and eating
and sleeping, friendships are
essential to our survival.

ADELAIDE BRY

Of all the things which wisdom provides
to make life entirely happy, much the greatest
is the possession of friendship.

EPICURUS (341-270 B.C.)

friendships are essential
to our survival

ONE CAN DO WITHOUT PEOPLE,
BUT ONE HAS NEED OF A FRIEND.

CHINESE PROVERB

Aristotle's Essay on Friendship

Without friends no one would choose to live,
though he had all other goods; even rich people,
and those in possession of office and of dominating
power are thought to need friends most of all; for what
is the use of such prosperity without the opportunity
of beneficence, which is exercised chiefly and in its
most laudable form towards friends? Or how can
prosperity be guarded and preserved without friends?
The greater it is, the more exposed it is to risk.
And in poverty and in other misfortunes people
think friends are the only refuge. It helps the young,
too, to keep from error; it aids older people by
ministering to their needs and supplementing
the activities that are failing from weakness;
those in the prime of life it stimulates to noble actions...
for with friends people are more able both
to think and to act.

ARISTOTLE (384-322 B.C.)

*So closely interwoven have been our lives,
our purposes, and experiences that, separated,
we have a feeling of incompleteness – united,
such strength of self-assertion that no ordinary
obstacles, differences, or dangers ever appear
to us insurmountable.*

ELIZABETH CADY STANTON

*Friendship is the only cement
that will ever hold the world together.*

WOODROW WILSON (1856-1924)

*Friendships
link and loop
and interweave
until they mesh
the world.*

CHARLOTTE GRAY, b.1937

When friends are real
they are not glass threads or frost-work,
but the solidest thing we know.

RALPH WALDO EMERSON (1803-1882)

friendships mesh the world

The whole world over women and girls escape the
monotonies, the drudgeries, of everyday existence –
along well-trodden tracks, laughing together at the river's
edge or in the market square, exchanging ribaldries
from balconies, resting for a moment from the blinding
sun or driving rain. A net of companionship encircling
the planet. Strength regained. Sympathies exchanged.
Bitterness turned to warmth. Life made endurable
in shared experience, in laughter and in courage.

PAM BROWN, b.1928

I said "friendship is
the greatest bond in the world",
and I had reason for it,
for it is all the bands that this world hath.

JEREMY TAYLOR (1613-1667),
FROM "OF THE NATURE AND OFFICES OF FRIENDSHIP"

FRIENDS, BOOKS,
A CHEERFUL HEART,
&
CONSCIENCE CLEAR
ARE THE MOST
CHOICE COMPANIONS
WE HAVE HERE.

WILLIAM MATHER

What seems to grow fairer to me as life
goes by is the love and the grace and tenderness
of it; not its wit and cleverness and grandeur
of knowledge – grand as knowledge is –
but just the laughter of children and the friendship
of friends, and the cozy talk by the fire,
and the sight of flowers, and the sound of music.

AUTHOR UNKNOWN

We don't need to ask each other.
We know the sort of play the other likes,
which books, what music.
We know each other's most-loved flower and scent.
We know each other's oddities.
And so each meeting is like coming home.

PAM BROWN, b.1928

my life's companion

We've been friends forever.
I suppose that can't be true.
There must have been a time
before we became friends
but I can't remember it.
You are in my first memory
and all my best memories ever since.

LINDA MACFARLANE

*A*H, HOW GOOD IT FEELS!
THE HAND OF
AN OLD FRIEND.

HENRY WADSWORTH LONGFELLOW
(1807-1882)

*It is great to have friends when
one is young, but indeed it is still
greater when one is getting old.
When we are young, friends are,
like everything else, a matter of
course. In the old days we know
what it means to have them.*

EDVARD GRIEG (1843-1907)

*What a wretched lot
of old shrivelled creatures
we shall be by-and-by.
Never mind – the uglier
we get in the eyes of others,
the lovelier we shall be
to each other.*

GEORGE ELIOT (MARY ANN EVANS)
(1819-1880)

All the summer evenings that we've drifted round your
garden, sniffing the stocks and moonlit roses.
All the winters we have sprawled beside your fire,
the curtains drawn against the swirling snow.
All the days we've shopped and walked and talked together.
All these things we've shared.
Our lives so interwoven that we can scarcely think of
life without each other.
Stay close even if distance should divide us.
I need your kindness and I need your company.

PAM BROWN, b.1928

May friendship like wine,
improve as time advances.
And may we always have old wine,
old friends, and young cares.

TRADITIONAL

Surely there is no more beautiful sight to see
in all this world – than the growth of two friends' natures
who, as they grow old together, are always fathoming
with newer needs, deeper depths of each other's life....

PHILLIPS BROOKS

The best rule of friendship is to keep
your heart a little softer than your head.

GEORGE SANTAYANA (1863-1952)

*Oh the comfort, the inexpressible comfort of
feeling safe with a person; having neither to
weigh thoughts nor measure words, but pouring
them all right out just as they are chaff and
grain together; certain that a faithful hand will
take and sift them, keep what is worth keeping,
and then, with the breath of kindness blow
the rest away.*

DINAH MARIA MULOCK CRAIK (1826-1887)

... THE COMFORT,
THE INEXPRESSIBLE
COMFORT OF FEELING
SAFE WITH A PERSON

A friend is someone, to whom you can say any jackass thing that enters your mind. With acquaintances, you are forever aware of their slightly unreal image of you, and you edit yourself to fit. Many marriages are between acquaintances. You can be with a person for three hours of your life and have a friend. Another one will remain an acquaintance for thirty years.

J.D. MACDONALD

First of all things, for friendship, there must be that delightful, indefinable state called feeling at ease with your companion, the one man, the one woman out of a multitude who interest you, who meets your thoughts and tastes.

JULIA DUHRING

By secrecy I mean you both want the habit of telling each other at the moment everything that happens – where you go – and what you do – that free communication of letters and opinions, just as they arise... which is after all the only groundwork of friendship....

MARY ANN LAMB

The world is so wide
and each of us so small –
yet bound by friendship
we are giants.

PAM BROWN, b.1928

Because I got you to look after me, and you got me to
look after you.... We got each other, that's what....

JOHN STEINBECK (1902-1968)

To fall down you manage alone but it takes
friendly hands to get up.

YIDDISH PROVERB

True friends, like ivy and the wall
Both stand together, and together fall.

FRANCIS BACON

Hold a true friend
with both your hands.

NIGERIAN PROVERB

*Two people holding each other up like
flying buttresses.
Two people depending on each other and
babying each other and defending
each other against the world.*

ERICA JONG, b.1942

*How often have we built each other as shelters
against the cold .*

AUDRE LORDE

Two people holding each other

*I love you not only
for what you are,
but for what I am
when I am with you.
I love you not only
for what you have made
of yourself, but for what you
are making of me.*

ROY CROFT

M_Y
BEST FRIEND
IS THE ONE
WHO BRINGS OUT
THE BEST IN ME.

HENRY FORD

No one can develop freely
in this world and find a full life
without feeling understood
by at least one person.

PAUL TOURNIER

What is a friend?
(I will tell you.)
It is a person with whom you dare to be yourself.

FRANK CRANE

A friend accepts you for who you are, but expects you to be
all you can be.

RICHARD LOUV, FROM "THE WEB OF LIFE"

Each friend represents a world in us,
a world possibly not born until they arrive,
and it is only by this meeting that
a new world is born.

ANAÏS NIN (1903-1977)

I want someone to laugh with me, someone to be grave
with me, someone to please me and help my
discrimination with his or her own remark, and at times,
no doubt to admire my acuteness and penetration.

ROBERT BURNS (1759-1796)

It is a mistake to think that one makes a friend because of his or her qualities, it has nothing to do with qualities at all. It is the person that we want, not what he does or says, or does not do or say, but what he or she is that is eternally enough! Who shall explain the extraordinary instinct that tells us, perhaps after a single meeting, that this or that particular person in some mysterious way matters to us? I confess that, for myself, I never enter a new company without the hope that I may discover a friend, perhaps the friend, sitting there with an expectant smile. That hope survives a thousand disappointments. People who deal with life generously and large-heartedly go on multiplying relationships in the end.

ARTHUR CHRISTOPHER BENSON (1862-1925)

One does not make friends;
one recognizes them.

ISABEL PATERSON

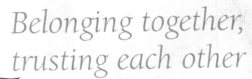

Belonging together, trusting each other

The very best thing is good talk,
and the thing that helps it most
is friendship.
How it dissolves the barriers
that divide us, and loosens all
constraints, and diffuses itself
like some fine old cordial
through all the veins of life –
this feeling that we understand
and trust each other, and wish
each other heartily well!

HENRY VAN DYKE

*Being with you is like walking on a clear morning
– definitely the sensation of belonging there.*

E.B. WHITE (1899-1985)

*He who, silent, loves
to be with us, and loves us
in our silence, has touched
one of the keys
that warm hearts.*

JOHN C. LAVATER

*There is no desire so deep as the simple desire for
companionship.*

GRAHAM GREENE (1904-1991)

No road is long with a friend at your side.

JAPANESE PROVERB

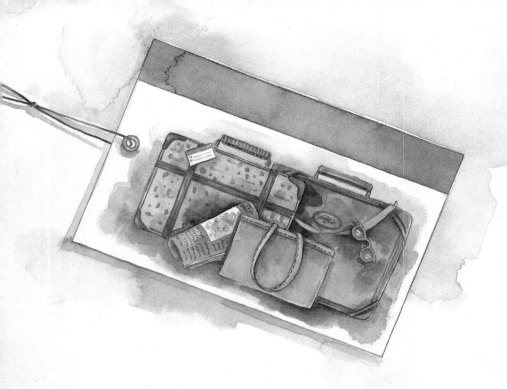

We live so far apart, and yet, somehow
we have kept track of one another.
Too long a silence and each begins to worry.
We need to know the other is there —
sharing the planet,
safe and sound, under the self-same star.
The link we fashioned so long ago is thin
as a thread but strong as steel.

PAM BROWN, b.1928

When a person that one loves
is in the world and alive and well...
then to miss them is only
a new flavour, a salt sharpness
in experience.

WINIFRED HOLTBY (1895-1935)

I never weary of watching for you
on the road.
Each day I go out to the city gate
With a flask of wine, lest you
should come thirsty.
Oh that I could shrink the surface
of the world,
so that suddenly I might find you
standing at my side.

WANG-CHIEN

A little more kindness, a little less creed,
A little more giving, a little less greed,
A little more smile, a little less frown,
A little less kicking a man when he's down,
A little more "we", and a little less "I",
A little more laugh, a little less cry,
A little more flowers on the pathway of life,
And fewer on graves at the end of the strife.

AUTHOR UNKNOWN

There are times in life
when you most need friends.
On standby.
Ready to do anything or go anywhere.
Thank you for doing,
being, just that.

PAM BROWN, b.1928

The balm of life,
a kind and faithful friend.

MERCY OTIS WARREN
(1728-1814)

Little kindnesses repeated
a thousand times
have the greatest value.

PUSHPA PATEL

Do not keep the alabaster boxes of your love and tenderness sealed up until your friends are dead. Fill their lives with sweetness. Speak approving cheering words while their ears can hear them and while their hearts can be thrilled by them.

GEORGE W. CHILDS

Ships that pass in the night, and speak to each other in passing,
Only a signal shown, and a distant voice in the darkness;
So on the ocean of life, we pass and speak to one another,
Only a look and a voice, then darkness again and a silence.

HENRY WADSWORTH LONGFELLOW (1807-1882)

The comfort of having a friend
may be taken away,
but not that of having had one.

SENECA (4B.C.–65A.D.)

I think there is, in friendship,
an instant recognition –
a kind of loving.
It needs just a word, in passing,
the touch of a hand –
yet parting is loss and the tiny ache
of regret stays with us always.

HELEN M. EXLEY

WHEREVER YOU
ARE IT IS YOUR
OWN FRIENDS
WHO MAKE YOUR
WORLD.

WILLIAM JAMES
(1842-1910)

connections
across the world

Our different homes perhaps a continent apart.
All my dear friends. Known only for a brief time
and sometimes so long ago,
but alive forever in my mind and heart.

HELEN THOMSON, b.1943

To know someone here or there
with whom you feel there is understanding
in spite of distances or thoughts unexpressed –
that can make of this earth a garden.

JOHANN WOLFGANG VAN GOETHE (1749-1832)

Happiness is the whole world
as friends. It's light all
through your life.

DANIEL DILLING, AGE 8

To love and to be loved, is the greatest happiness.
If I lived under the burning sun of the equator,
it would be pleasure for me to think that there
may be many human beings on the other side
of the world who regarded and respected me;
I could not live if I were alone upon the earth,
and cut off from the rememberance of
my fellow creatures.

SYDNEY SMITH (1771-1845)

through our lives together

*To the young, friendship comes as the glory
of the spring, a very miracle of beauty,
a mystery of birth: to the old it has
the bloom of autumn, beautiful still.*

HUGO BLACK

*There is no friend like the old friend
who has shared our morning days,
No greeting like his welcome,
no homage like his praise;
Fame is the scentless sunflower,
with gaudy crown of gold;
But friendship is the breathing rose,
with sweets in every fold.*

OLIVER WENDELL HOLMES (1809-1894)

*Wishing to be friends is quick work,
but friendship is a slow-ripening fruit.*

ARISTOTLE (384-322 B.C.)

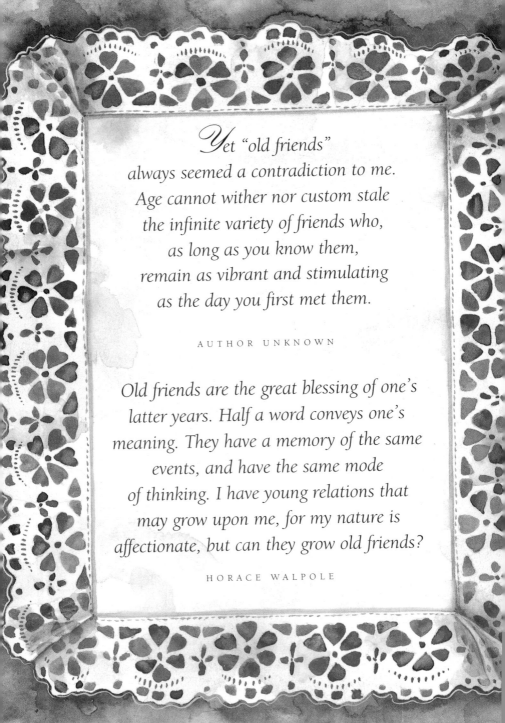

*Yet "old friends"
always seemed a contradiction to me.
Age cannot wither nor custom stale
the infinite variety of friends who,
as long as you know them,
remain as vibrant and stimulating
as the day you first met them.*

AUTHOR UNKNOWN

*Old friends are the great blessing of one's
latter years. Half a word conveys one's
meaning. They have a memory of the same
events, and have the same mode
of thinking. I have young relations that
may grow upon me, for my nature is
affectionate, but can they grow old friends?*

HORACE WALPOLE

When we were very small we played together

under the summer trees, picked dandelions to carry home,

drew in the dust of shadowed lanes, stamped in mud,

kicked joyfully through Autumn leaves.

Age was no concern of ours. The seasons gave their gifts

and gave no hint that time would mark us.

But trees are felled, the meadows vanished,

the lanes forgotten. And we are growing old, my friend.

Walk with me, then, and talk of those lost times –

still vivid in our minds. Still living in our hearts.

Life is still good – but we live in both worlds.

We recognise the children that we were

shining in one another's eyes.

And smile – knowing that nothing good is ever lost.

PAM BROWN, b.1928

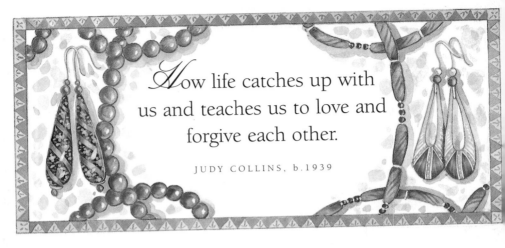

How life catches up with
us and teaches us to love and
forgive each other.

JUDY COLLINS, b.1939

If the first law of friendship is that
it has to be cultivated,
the second law is to be
indulgent when the first law
has been neglected.

VOLTAIRE (1694-1778)

It's always amazing what a friend can forgive.

AUTHOR UNKNOWN

accepting, forgivir

𝒯hank you for simply accepting me as I am.
No need to act.
You know my faults and sigh and smile – and are my friend.

PAM BROWN, b.1928

I always felt that the great high privilege,
relief and comfort of friendship
was that one had to explain nothing.

KATHERINE MANSFIELD (1888-1923)

I love you for ignoring the possibilities of the fool and the
weakling in me, and for laying firm
hold on the possibilities of the good in me.

ROY CROFT

One is taught by experience to put a premium on those few
people who can appreciate you for what you are...

GAIL GODWIN, b.1937

ch other

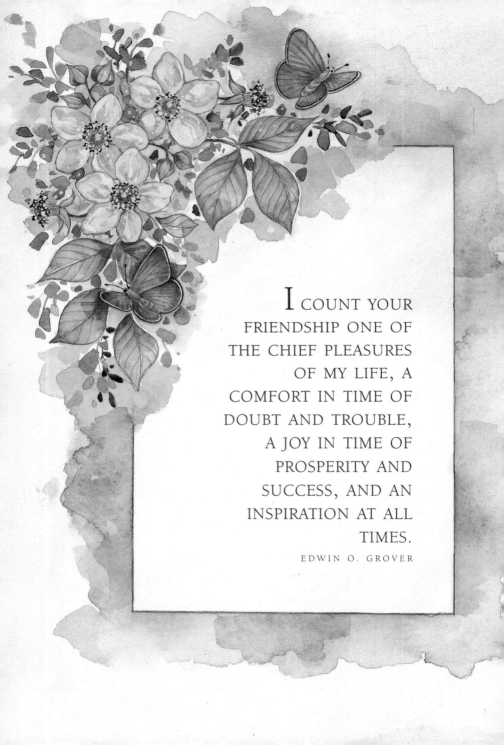

I COUNT YOUR
FRIENDSHIP ONE OF
THE CHIEF PLEASURES
OF MY LIFE, A
COMFORT IN TIME OF
DOUBT AND TROUBLE,
A JOY IN TIME OF
PROSPERITY AND
SUCCESS, AND AN
INSPIRATION AT ALL
TIMES.

EDWIN O. GROVER

In a thousand ways [my friends]
have turned my limitations into beautiful privileges,
and enabled me to walk serene
and happy in the shadow cast by my deprivation.

HELEN KELLER (1880-1968)

There is no love so good and so powerful
as the one you find expressed in friendship.

SIR LAURENS VAN DER POST (1906-1996)

When we come into contact with our friend we enter into a
different environment where the air we breathe is more pure,
the sounds we hear are sharper, the colors we see more
dramatic, and the ideas we think quicker and more insightful.
The physical environment is completely different, because now
we are in a situation not only where we are free to be
ourselves but where we have no choice.

ANDREW M. GREELEY, b.1928
FROM "THE FRIENDSHIP GAME"

When I see him I feel the joy deep inside me,
like a pilgrim who is lost and finds the right way at last.

G. LAENEN

Thank you for sitting very still and nodding

in all the right places when I told you

some tale of injustice and wrong doing

and worked myself to fever pitch.

And making me a cup of tea when I had quite done.

PAM BROWN, b.1928

LISTENING

You can't fake listening.
It shows.

RAQUEL WELCH, b.1942

The friends who listen to us
are the ones we move toward,
and we want to sit in their radius.
When we are listened to, it creates us,
makes us unfold and expand.

KARL MENNIGER

"Stay" is a charming word
in a friend's vocabulary.

LOUISA MAY ALCOTT (1832-1888)

They took my couch and placed it in the setting sun;
They spread my rug and I leaned on the balcony-pillar.
Tranquil talk was better than any medicine;
Gradually the feelings came back to my numbed heart.

PO CHU-I (772-846),
TRANSLATED BY ARTHUR WALEY (1889-1966)

Life's true wealth

*A poor man may be said
to be rich in the midst of his poverty
so long as he enjoys the interior
sunshine of a devoted friend.
The wealthiest of men,
on the contrary,
is poor and miserable, if he has
no friend whom he can grasp
by the hand, and to whom
he can disclose the secrets
of his heart.*

JAMES GIBBONS
(1834-1921)

*Money can buy many things,
good and evil.
All the wealth of the world
could not buy you a friend
or pay you for the loss of one.*

G.D. PRENTICE

A faithful friend is a secure shelter;
Whoever finds one has found a treasure.
A faithful friend is beyond price;
His worth is more than money can buy.
A faithful friend is an elixir of life....

ECCLESIASTES

It is a good thing to be rich, and a good thing to be
strong, but it is a better thing to be loved of many
friends.

EURIPIDIES (c.485-406 B.C.)

... solid friends really are one of the riches of life.

JERRY HALL

Deft thieves can break your locks and carry off your
savings, fire consume your home...
fortune can't take away what you give your friends: that
wealth stays yours forever.

MARCUS MARTIAL (c.40-c.104)

WISE SAYINGS OFTEN FALL ON BARREN GROUND;
BUT A KIND WORD IS NEVER THROWN AWAY.

SIR ARTHUR HELPS (1813-1875)

for your deep kindness

THE HAPPINESS OF LIFE
IS MADE UP OF MINUTE FRACTIONS —
THE LITTLE SOON-FORGOTTEN
CHARITIES
OF A KISS, A SMILE,
A KIND LOOK,
A HEARTFELT COMPLIMENT.

SAMUEL TAYLOR COLERIDGE
(1772-1834)

For your deep kindness, great thanks.

HELEN FITZWALTER-READ

It is the small, insignificant,
simple gestures that make life bearable.
A smile, a touch, a word, a kindness,
a concern.

PAM BROWN, b.1928

For whoever knows how to return a kindness
he has received must be a friend above all price.

SOPHOCLES (469-406 B.C.)

A look of sympathy, of encouragement;
a hand reached out in kindness.
And all else is secondary.

MAYA V. PATEL, b.1943

... there can be no happiness equal to the joy of finding a heart that understands.

VICTOR ROBINSON

$\mathcal{T}$he language of friendship
is not words, but meanings.
It is an intelligence
above language.

HENRY DAVID THOREAU
(1817-1862)

... when two people are at one in their inmost hearts,
They shatter even the strength of iron or bronze.
And when two people understand each other in their inmost hearts,
Their words are sweet and strong, like the fragrance of orchids.

CONFUCIUS, FROM "FELLOWSHIP WITH MEN" (551-479 B.C.)

... True Blue Friends... make you feel good
and warm; they are automatically on
the same wavelength....

ADELAIDE BRY

understanding each other

Old friends are best.
King James used to call for his old shoes;
they were easiest for his feet.

JOHN SELDON (1584-1654)

My coat and I live comfortably together.
It has assumed all my wrinkles,
does not hurt me anywhere,
has moulded itself on to my deformities,
and is complacent to all my movements,
and I only feel its presence
because it keeps me warm.
Old friends and old coats are the same thing.

VICTOR HUGO

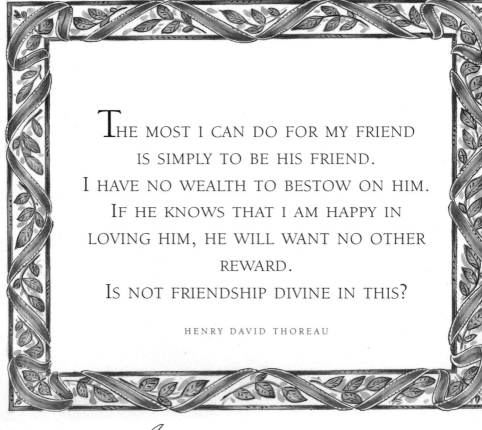

THE MOST I CAN DO FOR MY FRIEND
IS SIMPLY TO BE HIS FRIEND.
I HAVE NO WEALTH TO BESTOW ON HIM.
IF HE KNOWS THAT I AM HAPPY IN
LOVING HIM, HE WILL WANT NO OTHER
REWARD.
IS NOT FRIENDSHIP DIVINE IN THIS?

HENRY DAVID THOREAU

And all people live, not for reason
of any care they have for themselves,
but by the love for them
that is in other people.

LEO TOLSTOY (1828-1910)

Being a friend, I do not care, not I.
How gods or men wrong me, beat me down.
His words are a sufficient star to travel by.
I count him with quiet praise.
Being a friend, I do not covet gold,
Or the royal gift to give him pleasure, but,
sit with him and have him hold my hand.

AIDS PATIENT

simply to be his friend

*Friendship is unnecessary,
like philosophy, like art....
It has no survival value;
rather it is one of those things
that give value to survival.*

C.S. LEWIS (1898-1963)

... when the whole world has gone out

A friend is one who comes in
when the whole world has gone out.

ALBAN GOODIER

When I've felt I could not weather some apparent disaster, you have stood beside me and told me that I can. And I have.

CLARA ORTEGA, b.1955

Our friendships are... the structures that hold us in place when our world threatens to disolve.

EURIPIDES (484-406 B.C.)

To have even one good friend is to keep the darkness at bay.

PAM BROWN, b.1928

It is not that a person has occasion often to fall back on the kindness of friends; perhaps we may never experience the necessity of doing so; but we are governed by our imaginations, and they stand there as a solid and impregnable bulwark against the evils of life.

SYDNEY SMITH (1771-1845)

True happiness consists not in the multitude of friends,
But in the worth and choice.

BEN JONSON (1572-1637)

*I remember the early days... when you used to say
"I hope you won't be offended..." When you brought over
hand-on children's clothes or half a chocolate cake.
I never was, of course and it developed into a two-way
traffic – my apples, your cabbages, my scones, your
shortbread. And now I'm trotting over to your back door
with out-grown baby clothes for your grandchildren.
We've made a good team, you and I!*

PAM BROWN, b.1928

*If true friendship can be found, cherish it like
a fine gem. Polish it, go out of your way
to keep and protect it. Keep it safe.*

MARY SWANEY

Happy to whom, in maturer season of life, there remains one tired and constant friend.

AUTHOR UNKNOWN

Then little by little we discover one friend, in the midst of the crowd of friends, who is particularly happy to be with us and to whom, we realize, we have an infinite number of things to say. She is not the top of the class, she is not particularly well thought of by the others, she does not wear showy clothes... and when we are walking home we realize that her shoes are identical to ours — strong and simple, not showy and flimsy like those of our other friends....

NATALIA GINZBURG, b.1916
FROM "THE LITTLE VIRTUES"

one constant friend

Real friends are those who, when you've made a fool of yourself, don't feel you've done a permanent job.

AUTHOR UNKNOWN

We need someone to believe in us

— if we do well,

we want our work commended,

our faith corroborated.

The individual who thinks well of you, who keeps his

mind on your good qualities, and does not look for

your flaws, is your friend.

Who is my brother?

I'll tell you:

he is one who recognizes good in me.

ELBERT HUBBARD

Thank you for showing me
that being made to look ridiculous
isn't the end of the world.

PAM BROWN, b.1928

It costs nothing to say a "hello" here and there.
To friends that you pass in the street.
It costs nothing to smile at a stranger,
Or at any new friend that you meet.
It costs nothing to show your emotions,
or your feelings when things don't go right.
It costs nothing to help the unfortunate,
Who are blind or who have no sight.
It costs nothing to be happy.
And happiness can be found.
Happiness is like butter,
So go on and spread some around.

JEANETTE ACHILLES, AGE 15

HAPPINESS SEEMS MADE TO BE SHARED.

JEAN RACINE (1639-1699)

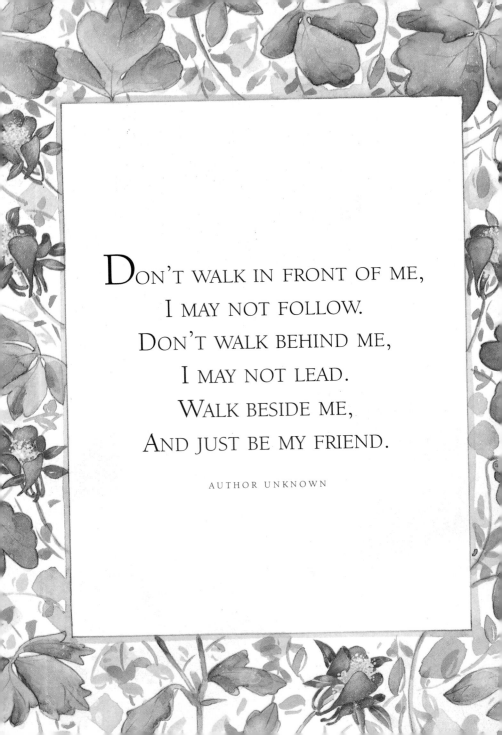

Don't walk in front of me,
I may not follow.
Don't walk behind me,
I may not lead.
Walk beside me,
And just be my friend.

AUTHOR UNKNOWN

I have had many friends
that time and distance,
change and loss have swept away.
I hold their memory,
flowers pressed between the days
— and breathing still the scent
of distant summers.
But some remain —
deep-rooted in my life
and bright with living blossom.
A constant comfort and a constant joy.

PAM BROWN, b.1928

Some people come into our lives
and quickly go...
Some people stay a while
and leave their footprints on our hearts,
and we are never,
ever the same.

FLAVIA

When friendship once is
rooted fast
It is a plant
no storm can blast.

FROM A 19TH CENTURY
CALLING CARD

I want to be your friend
For ever and ever without break or decay.
When the hills are all flat
And the rivers are all dry,
When it lightens and thunders in winter,
When it rains and snows in summer,
When heaven and earth mingle
Not till then will I part from you.

CHINESE OATH OF FRIENDSHIP, 1ST CENTURY